THE EVERY BODY BOOK

The LGBTQ+ Inclusive Guide for Kids about Sex,
Gender, Bodies, and Families

Rachel E. Simon, LCSW, MEd

Illustrated by Noah Grigni

Jessica Kingsley Publishers
London and Philadelphia

First published in 2020
by Jessica Kingsley Publishers
73 Collier Street
London N1 9BE, UK
and
400 Market Street, Suite 400
Philadelphia, PA 19106, USA

www.jkp.com

Front cover image source: Noah Grigni.
Typeset by Adam Peacock.

Library of Congress Cataloging in Publication Data
A CIP catalog record for this book is available from the Library of Congress

British Library Cataloguing in Publication Data
A CIP catalogue record for this book is available from the British Library

ISBN 978 1 78775 173 6
eISBN 978 1 78775 174 3

Printed and bound in China

TABLE OF CONTENTS

To M, a total rockstar, and her amazing family

INTRODUCTION: WHY THIS BOOK, WHY NOW (A NOTE FOR THE GROWN-UPS)

How many children's books have you seen about sex, gender, bodies, and families? Of those books, how many of them truly reflect the diversity of human bodies, identities, and how we choose to connect with one another? In my experience as a clinical psychotherapist and sexuality educator, I have heard over and over from children and their families how much anxiety exists in finding resources to help facilitate exploration of these concepts. As preteens and teens come into their identities, they and their families need resources to help navigate tough and crucial conversations about sex. My hope with this book is to provide an inclusive view of sexuality that neither I nor my clients have seen in other children's books on the subject.

Talking about sexuality should be something that happens consistently over the course of a child's development. Challenging the notion of "The Talk" and instead opening a path to recurring topics of discussion can be a unique mission. It can be uncomfortable for you or uncomfortable for your child—probably both. But the more comfort you can build into talking about sexuality, the better informed your children will be about their own health, values, and choices. Talking about sex in a way that models healthy attitudes and creates an atmosphere of openness allows your child to grow into a happy, healthy, sexually empowered adult. We want children to internalize those attitudes now, so they later feel prepared and confident. Avoiding talking about sex sends a message of shame, discomfort, and secrecy.

In the age of the internet, when the vast majority of kids and teens list "online" as their main source of sexuality information, parents can be a crucial component of how their kids are set up for success in sexual decision making. Opening and encouraging channels of communication can help your child feel comfortable coming to you with a question or a problem. Although this book can be read together, your child may want to read some chapters alone, which is totally normal. Many adults have not had the comprehensive sexuality education that they needed when they were younger, and this book will be helpful for age-appropriate explanations of tough concepts!

You will notice that in this book I use a lot of gender-neutral language—such as "parent" instead of "mother," and "person with a penis" instead of "male." The reason I do this is to be inclusive of people along the entire spectrum of gender identity. Yes, many people with vaginas are women, but some are not. It is important for our children to learn about themselves and about the experiences of kids who are different from them. I am hopeful that using inclusive language can help teach children of all genders (while reminding ourselves) that sex and gender are two different things, that transgender, non-binary, and intersex people deserve representation and affirmation, and that we can make people feel safe just by welcoming them with our words (more on this in Chapter 2).

This is a book for all kinds of kids and all kinds of families. I hope that it provides information in a safe, inclusive, affirming way, and that it helps jumpstart important conversations in your family and community.

CHAPTER 1

SEX?! WHAT'S THAT?

Even though it only has three letters, SEX can be a BIG word! When people use the word *sex*, they can be talking about a bunch of different things. Sex has to do with the body parts people have, how babies are made, the physical acts of showing love and feeling pleasure, and so much more. Sexuality can include how we feel about our bodies, what choices we make, who we want to be close to or intimate with, and the emotions that we feel. Human sexuality can affect us in different ways throughout our whole lives!

Even though sexuality is so important, it can be hard or awkward to talk about—and sometimes people tell us we shouldn't talk about it at all. But it's totally normal to be curious about sex, and to have lots of questions. Who wouldn't have lots of questions about something like that? It is also okay to talk about sex with certain people in safe places. Many kids your age wonder how babies are made, what sex is, and what will happen to their bodies as they go through puberty and change from a kid to a grown-up.

You might hear about sex at school, on TV, online, or in many other places. Learning about sex, bodies, babies, families, and sexual health is important. Having more information can help us to take care of our bodies, keep ourselves safe, and make important choices. You may feel curious or excited about sex. You may also feel confused or embarrassed about sex. You might notice that you want more privacy for your body, and privacy to learn more about sex. Whatever you feel is okay, and talking with someone you trust is a great way to start getting some of your questions answered. So is reading this book!

Growing up and finding out new information can be both exciting and scary. You might have to think about this information for a while, and you might have lots of feelings as you learn. There are no silly questions about sex, and there are people who can help you understand with accurate information and no judgment. Some of the adults that can help you are your parents, doctors, nurses, teachers, or other family members. Another place where some of us go for information is the internet. If you're looking for answers to sexuality questions on the internet, it's important to ask an adult for help finding a safe website for kids.

You might also find a lot of answers right here in this book!

CHAPTER 2

SEX AND GENDER

When babies are born, one of the first questions people ask is whether the baby is a boy or a girl. They are actually asking about the *biological sex* of the baby. Biological sex is assigned, or labeled, when babies are born, based on the visible body parts they have. Lots of our body parts are the same, no matter what sex we are. Most of us have arms and legs, fingers and toes, eyes, noses, and mouths, too. Our genitals, which are the private parts between our legs, are different! If a baby has a penis, the baby is assigned male. If a baby has a vulva, the baby is assigned female.

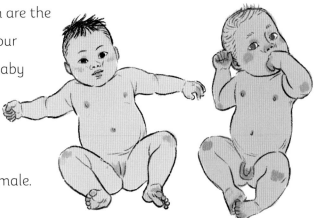

There are also differences inside the bodies of babies with different biological sexes. There are *chromosomes*, which contain the genes that babies get from their parents. Babies who are assigned female have different chromosomes from babies that are assigned male.

What are *genes*? Genes are instructions for how the body is formed. We get genes from our biological parents! They are a roadmap for how the body is put together.

There are also *hormones*, which are chemicals inside our bodies that influence how babies develop. Babies who are assigned female have hormones that are different from babies that are assigned male.

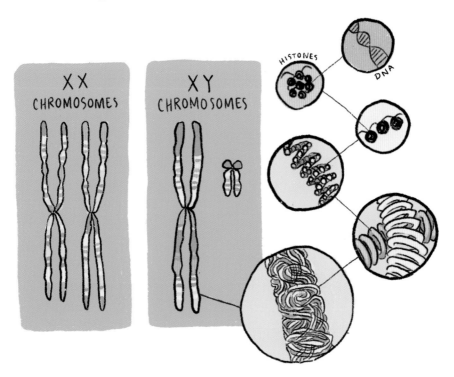

Most people are assigned "male" and "female" for their biological sex. However, some babies are born *intersex*. That means they are born with bodies that aren't easily defined as "male" or "female." These babies might have some body parts that doctors expect to find on bodies assigned male, and some body parts that doctors expect to find on bodies assigned female. Depending on whether or not these differences are on the outside or inside of the body, doctors might know if someone is intersex when they are born, during puberty, or even later in life. Remember: biological sex has to do with what our bodies are like on the inside and outside, but it doesn't have to do with whether we *feel* like a boy or girl or neither.

Gender is different from biological sex. Gender involves society's expectations about how girls and boys are supposed to behave and express themselves. Gender can be complicated! It has to do with our roles, our identities, our legal status as male, female, or non-binary, and the way we communicate. Our *gender identity* is how we identify ourselves in our hearts and our minds—girl, boy, neither, or somewhere in between. Knowing how much you feel like a girl, boy, or other gender is really clear for some kids, while others take lots of time and thinking to figure it out. What do you think of your gender? Do you have words you like to use to describe your identity?

When our gender identity matches the biological sex assigned to us at birth, it is called being *cisgender*. If you have a vulva and identify as a girl, you are a cisgender girl or woman. If you have a penis and identify as a boy, you are a cisgender boy or man.

Some people who are born with penises don't identify as boys or as male—they might feel more like a girl or another gender. Some people born with vulvas don't identify as girls or as female. When our gender identity does not match the biological sex assigned to us at birth, it is called being *transgender*.

Being cisgender ("cis") or transgender ("trans") isn't a choice—just like some people are left-handed or have curly hair or freckles, it's another way we can be different. It's just who we are!

Some people identify as a boy or as a girl. Others identify sometimes as a boy, and sometimes as a girl, and sometimes both. And some people don't feel like a boy or a girl at all. *Non-binary* is a word to describe genders that are not "boy" or "girl." *Pronouns* are the words we use when talking about a boy, a girl, or a non-binary person. Some people like to use "he and him" pronouns, some like to use "she and her," and some people like to use "they and them." What's most important is to respect who people are, what they want to be called, and understand that this is what makes them feel best on the inside. Calling someone by the wrong pronouns can be very hurtful and is called *misgendering*.

Some people think there is only one way to be a boy or a girl, and that your biological sex and your gender identity are the same thing. But we know that this isn't true! We all have a gender identity as well as a biological sex. Since babies can't talk, they can't tell us their genders yet! We only know their assigned biological sex. Some people who are transgender know it as soon as they can talk. Others realize it later in their lives. Some people have a gender identity that is *fluid* and can change throughout their lives. When someone tells us their gender identity, we should be respectful and use the names and pronouns that they use.

There are lots of ways to be a girl or a boy or another gender whether you are cis or trans! *Gender expression* is how we show our gender to the world. We do this with our clothes, our hairstyle, our accessories, and lots more. Some of the words we use about gender expression are *feminine*, *masculine*, and *androgynous*. Androgynous means being somewhere in between masculine and feminine. This is something lots of kids explore. There is no wrong way to express being a boy, a girl, or anything in between! For some people, gender expression can be fluid and change from day to day. For other people, gender expression is something that stays the same a lot of the time. Remember, we can't tell someone's gender identity, or their pronouns, just from how they express their gender.

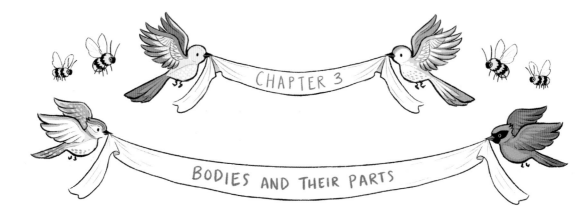

Vulvas can belong to people who are cisgender girls and women, but they can also belong to people who are transgender boys and men, and non-binary people too! People who have vulvas are usually assigned female at birth.

These bodies are born with parts called ovaries that make the eggs needed to make babies. When a person with ovaries is born, that person has all the eggs they will ever need to make babies.

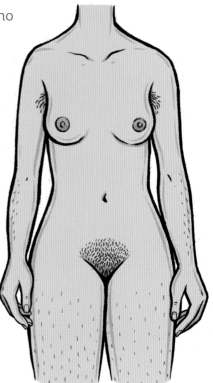

Penises can belong to people who are cisgender boys and men, but they can also belong to people who are transgender girls and women, and non-binary people too! People who have penises are usually assigned male at birth.

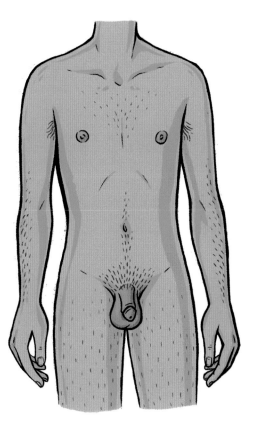

These bodies are born with parts that can make millions of sperm, which are needed to make a baby. Sperm are made in the testicles. When a person with testicles grows up, sperm is made in the testicles every day!

Everyone has some parts outside and some parts inside that we use every day to go to the bathroom. These parts can also help make a baby once our bodies are all grown up.

Here are the inside parts:

- The *vagina* is a passage that has an opening between the legs and goes up to the uterus.
- The *hymen* is a thin tissue that surrounds the opening of the vagina.
- The *uterus* is made of strong muscles and is where babies grow during pregnancy.
- The *cervix* is a small opening connecting the vagina and the uterus.
- The *fallopian tubes* are two narrow tubes that lead from the uterus to the ovaries.
- The *ovaries* are where eggs are stored, and they develop during puberty.
- The *urethra* is a little tube that goes from the bladder to a tiny opening between someone's legs. It is a different opening from the vagina. We use the urethra to pee.
- The *bladder* is an organ that stores urine.

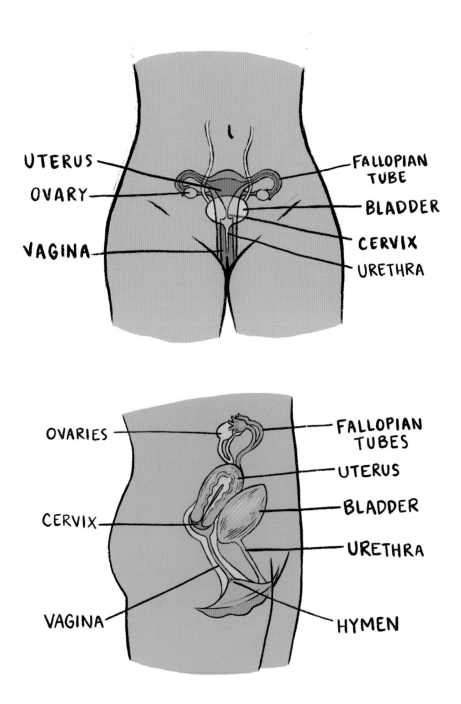

UTERUS

OVARY

VAGINA

FALLOPIAN TUBE

BLADDER

CERVIX

URETHRA

OVARIES

CERVIX

VAGINA

FALLOPIAN TUBES

UTERUS

BLADDER

URETHRA

HYMEN

- The *penis* is made of spongy tissue that is able to make the penis hard and soft at different times.
- The *urethra* is a little tube that is inside the penis and leads up to the *bladder*. We use the urethra to pee.
- The *bladder* is an organ that stores urine.
- The *prostate* is a gland that makes fluid to help nourish and protect sperm cells, and helps the sperm get to the urethra.
- The *seminal vesicles*, along with the prostate, make a milky fluid called *semen*, which helps nourish sperm cells.
- The *epididymis* is a long tube that is connected to the side of the testicle. There are two of these tubes, one for each testicle.
- The *bulbourethral glands* (*Cowper's glands*) provide more lubricating fluid to help sperm move through the urethra.
- The *vas deferens* is a narrow tube that takes sperm and semen from the epididymis to the urethra. There are also two of these tubes, one for each testicle.
- The *scrotum* is a sac of skin that protects and holds the two testicles.
- The *testicles* make sperm once puberty begins. They also produce testosterone (see Chapter 4)!

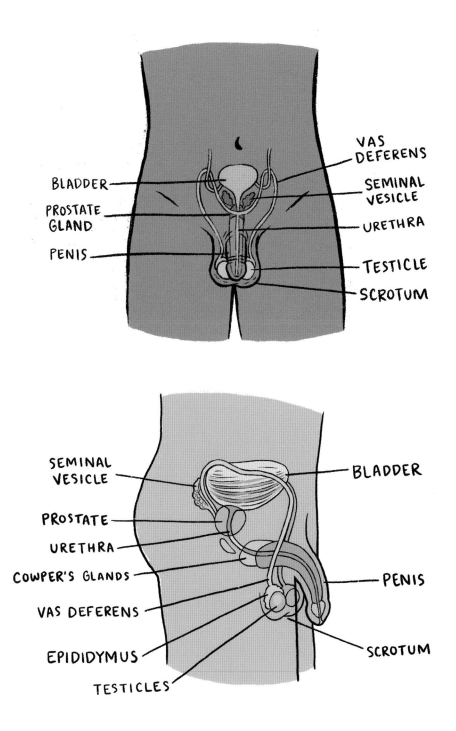

VAS
DEFERENS

SEMINAL
VESICLE

BLADDER

URETHRA

PROSTATE
GLAND

PENIS

TESTICLE

SCROTUM

SEMINAL
VESICLE

BLADDER

PROSTATE

URETHRA

COWPER'S GLANDS

VAS DEFERENS

PENIS

EPIDIDYMUS

SCROTUM

TESTICLES

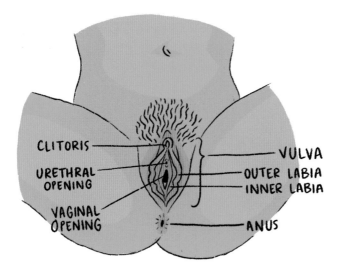

CLITORIS
URETHRAL OPENING
VAGINAL OPENING

VULVA
OUTER LABIA
INNER LABIA
ANUS

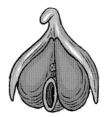

INTERNAL STRUCTURE OF CLITORIS

This is what's on the outside:

- The *vulva* is the soft area between the legs. Lots of people call the vulva the vagina by mistake!

- The vulva includes the *inner* and *outer labia*, two folds of skin that protect the inside of the vulva.

- The *clitoris* is a small and sensitive nub of tissue and nerve endings at the top of the vulva that also extends inside the body.

- There are two openings in the vulva: the *urethral opening* and the *vaginal opening*. The urethra is where urine comes out. The vagina is where most babies come out (more about birth in Chapter 9)!

- Behind the vulva is the *anus*, an opening where feces, also called poop, comes out.

UNCIRCUMCIZED

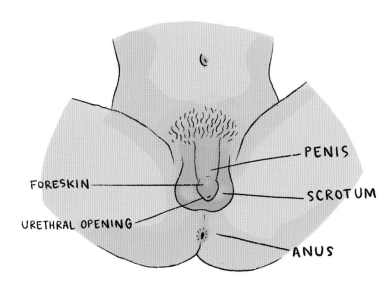

PENIS

FORESKIN

SCROTUM

URETHRAL OPENING

ANUS

CIRCUMCIZED

- The *penis* hangs in front of the scrotum and has a small opening at the tip for urine to come out. This is called the *urethral opening*. Semen also comes out from the tip of the penis, but never at the same time as urine!

- The *scrotum* is a soft and squishy sac that holds the testicles. The scrotum keeps the testicles protected and at the right temperature to make sperm.

- The *foreskin* is a layer of skin over the end of the penis. Some people have their foreskin removed in a process called "circumcision." This is often done a few days after a baby is born by a doctor or a trained religious person. Some people do not have their foreskin removed. Both kinds of penis are normal.

- Behind the scrotum is the *anus*, an opening where feces, also called poop, comes out.

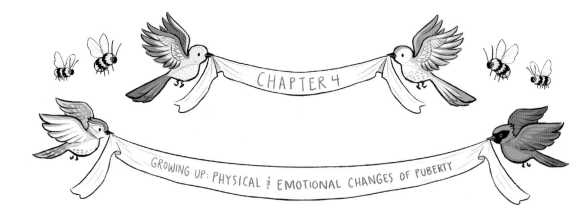

CHAPTER 4

GROWING UP: PHYSICAL & EMOTIONAL CHANGES OF PUBERTY

Between the ages of about 9 and 16, a lot of physical and emotional changes happen to us. This is called *puberty*, the time in young people's lives when their bodies begin to mature and change to look more like adult bodies. This is also the time when your body becomes able to make a baby by developing mature sperm or egg cells.

TWO HUMANS AGING

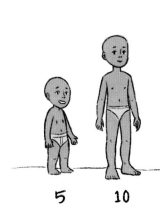

5   10   15   20   40   80

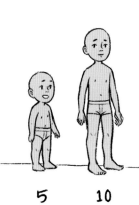

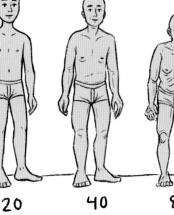
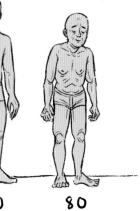

5   10   15   20   40   80

People with vaginas generally start puberty between age 9 and 11 with the development of breast buds that usually grow into larger breasts, which is followed by *menstruation*. Menstruation is something that happens every month if the egg does not meet sperm. Because the egg and sperm do not meet, no baby is made. When someone is menstruating, the uterus sheds its lining and blood comes out of the vagina for a few days. This flow of blood is called *menstruation*. It is also called having or getting a *period*.

This blood is not a sign of being sick or hurt, but is a normal cycle in bodies that make eggs. Menstrual blood can come in different shades of pink, red, brown, or black. Some people have very light periods while some people have heavier periods that produce more blood. Young people's periods can take a few years to become regular and consistent each month. People who menstruate might use pads in their underwear to absorb the blood, or they might use tampons, which are absorbent pieces of cotton that are inserted into the vagina. They might also use a menstrual cup, which is inserted into the vagina to catch menstrual blood.

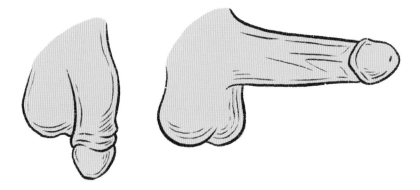

People with penises start puberty a little bit later, which usually begins with the development of pubic hair and the testicles getting bigger. Sometimes the penis stands up from the body and becomes large and hard. This is called an *erection*. It is normal and healthy for people with penises to have erections at any age. After puberty begins, and the testicles start making sperm, semen can sometimes come out of the penis during an erection. This is called *ejaculation*. To prepare for ejaculation, the body produces a drop of fluid that comes out of the penis during an erection to clear the way for semen to come out. Erections and ejaculation are normal and happen often in puberty.

Another thing that can happen in puberty is a *wet dream*, which is when someone has an erection in their sleep and semen comes out of their penis. People with vulvas can also have sexual dreams.

Many people start having sexual feelings during puberty. For others, sexual feelings may take longer to occur, or they may never be experienced at all. People of any gender might start thinking about sex more, and their bodies can get excited when they are doing things like watching a romantic scene in a movie or reading a romantic book.

Some people start exploring their bodies more during puberty, and when they touch their own genitals, they realize that it feels good. Really young kids explore their bodies, too, and adults often remind kids that touching their genitals is something that happens in private and not in front of other people.

Masturbation, or touching your own genitals for pleasure, is a totally normal thing for people to do privately. Masturbation can teach people about their bodies and what feels good to them. It cannot hurt you. It is normal if you want to masturbate, and it is also normal if you do not want to masturbate. Your body belongs to you, and you get to make your own personal decisions about masturbation.

Once puberty starts, changes take place over the next few years. They don't all start at once! You may have seen some older kids who have started puberty, and whose bodies are growing and looking more like adult bodies. *Hormones* are chemicals in our bodies that help our bodies do things like grow and change. When puberty starts, the hormones that tell our bodies to start changing and growing up increase. *Estrogen* is a hormone that helps develop changes in people with vulvas. *Testosterone* is a hormone that helps develop changes in people with penises. Everyone has both estrogen and testosterone, but at different levels. People who were assigned female at birth usually have more estrogen, and people assigned male at birth usually have more testosterone.

Some of the changes that can happen to people of all sexes during puberty are:

- growing taller
- gaining weight
- growing hair under arms, and on arms and legs, and pubic areas
- sweating more, increasing body odor
- getting pimples (acne) on their face and bodies
- new hormones being released.

Some changes that happen to people born with vulvas during puberty are:

- hips grow wider
- breasts grow larger (and sometimes one is bigger than the other)
- hair grows around the vulva
- vulva might have some clear or whitish discharge, or fluid
- ovaries start to release eggs
- menstruation begins.

Some changes that happen to people born with penises during puberty are:

- voice becomes deeper
- hair grows on upper lip, face, chest, and near the base of the penis
- testicles become larger and start to produce sperm
- more frequent erections (even when they're not thinking about sex).

Puberty is not the same for everyone, and it does not happen at the same speed. It can be hard to feel like the first person whose body is growing, and it can also be hard to feel like you're behind! People often feel self-conscious about what's happening to their body. Because of this—and because of the hormones— puberty can be a time when people have a lot of emotions. It's okay to feel sensitive, confused, lonely, and overwhelmed. We don't always like being in our bodies, and we might feel uncomfortable with the changes. Remember, people of all genders can feel uncomfortable in their bodies sometimes— body discomfort is not the same as being transgender.

The new hormones in our bodies during puberty might make it easier to move from happy to sad, or from confident to self-conscious really quickly! These quick changes in your mood are called *mood swings*. You might feel very sensitive, or irritable, or just weird and confused sometimes. You might find yourself thinking about your decisions, your values, and how you fit in with other people.

Be patient with yourself and with others, and find some supportive people to talk with about your feelings. If you find yourself experiencing a lot of sadness or anxiety, make sure that you try to talk about it with an adult. There's always help if you need it.

For transgender kids, it can be especially scary to feel that your body is physically changing in a way that does not match your gender identity. We use the words *gender dysphoria* to describe the discomfort a transgender person feels when their body feels different from how they feel in their head and their heart. Gender dysphoria is different from being uncomfortable with puberty—it can feel as if your body might be going through the wrong puberty! Kids who feel this way might talk to their parents and their doctors about using medicine called a *puberty blocker*.

Puberty blockers are like a big pause button for puberty. They stop the body from growing and changing in the ways that it is genetically programmed to change during puberty.

These blockers stop the creation of the hormones, estrogen and testosterone, that cause bodily changes such as breast growth, menstruation, hair growth, and voice-deepening. Trans, non-binary, and intersex kids might choose puberty blockers, or they might not. Whatever decisions people make with their families and their doctors are personal.

CHAPTER 5

LOVE AND ATTRACTION

Most people feel *attraction* for others. This means that they want to be close to, romantic with, or sexual with other people. *Sexual orientation* is how we describe who we are attracted to.

Heterosexual means you are attracted to someone of an opposite gender. Heterosexual men usually feel most attracted to women, and heterosexual women usually feel most attracted to men. The majority of people are heterosexual, which is also known as *straight*. But plenty of people are not straight, and there are many words to describe these many other sexual orientations.

One word we use to describe people who are not straight is *queer*. Some people use this word in a mean way, but others use it to describe their sexual orientation. Some of the queer identities include:

- **Gay**   People who are attracted to the same gender, AND men who are mostly or exclusively attracted to other men (previously known as homosexual, but most people prefer "gay").
- **Lesbian**   Women who are mostly or exclusively attracted to other women (sometimes use "gay").
- **Bisexual**   People who are attracted to people of their own gender and people of other genders.

- **Pansexual** People who are attracted to other people of all genders (some overlap with bisexual).
- **Questioning** People who are unsure or are still exploring their orientation.
- **Asexual** Some people do not experience sexual attraction to anyone. This is called being "asexual" or "ace" for short. This is a normal thing too!

Sometimes people use the acronym *LGBTQIA*, which stands for "lesbian, gay, bisexual, trans, queer or questioning, intersex, and asexual." You might see LGBTQIA with more letters, or a plus sign, to include even more sexual and gender identities!

Some people have a sense of their sexual orientations when they are young, but for others it can take much longer to know this part of themselves. Some people keep this information to themselves for a long time, before they *come out* and tell others. Sometimes people get messages that it's not okay to be gay or queer, but that's not true. Whoever you are or aren't attracted to is okay! Coming out can be a lifelong process for people who are not heterosexual and/or cisgender, and it is a very personal decision. Even though everyone has a gender identity and sexual orientation, LGBTQ+ people face pressure from our society to come out in a way that heterosexual and cisgender people do not. People can base the decision to come out on whether they feel safe and comfortable to share their identities with others in a certain situation.

Some people feel that being LGBTQIA is wrong. Sometimes those people call LGBTQIA people bad names and treat them disrespectfully. Some disapprove of these identities enough that they feel LGBTQIA people should not have the same rights to get married or adopt children as heterosexual or cisgender people. These people have been given misinformation that has caused them to fear people who are different from them. It is important to respect other people, no matter what their sexual orientation or gender identity.

For some people, attraction stays pretty much the same through their lives, but for others, attraction can be more *fluid* and can shift throughout their lives. This does not mean that straight people "turn" gay or that gay people can "turn" straight. Sexual orientation is not something that people can choose. But people can understand new things about themselves all the time.

No matter what your sexual orientation is, people who feel attracted to other people can experience things like butterflies, crushes, and feeling romantic and sexual love. You might feel a physical interest in someone, but you might also want to be emotionally close with them and be able to share thoughts and feelings too. Having a crush on someone can be exciting and confusing—you might not be sure whether you want to run and hide or be noticed by that person. Crushes can last for a day, a week, a month, or longer! Sometimes crushes turn into romantic love. Crushes can help us understand what things we like and don't like in another person.

CHAPTER 6

SEXUAL INTERCOURSE

The word "sex" can be used in lots of different ways. One of these ways is talking about "having sex." Much of the time, having sex is used to describe *sexual intercourse*. Sexual intercourse is what happens when people want their bodies to be close to each other emotionally and physically in a sexual way. Sex happens between people who are grown-ups.

People of any gender with any genitals can have sex together, when they want to be close to each other in a sexual way. The only type of sex that can form a baby, though, is with a penis (and sperm) and a vagina (and an egg). Some other types of sex can involve the mouth and the penis, the mouth and the vulva, and the penis and the anus.

Sex usually begins with two people kissing, hugging, caressing, touching, and feeling happy and connected. When this happens, bodies get aroused—penises become hard, or erect, and vaginas become slippery and wet. People who have sex move together with their bodies in a way that feels good. They continue to move their bodies, and sometimes people can have an *orgasm*. An orgasm is a feeling of releasing tension that bodies have when their touching is the most intense. It is sometimes called *climax*. A person with a penis often ejaculates semen during orgasm. This is what allows the sperm to travel from their body to another person's body to meet an egg. A person with a vagina feels their muscles tighten and relax over and over when they have an orgasm. Orgasms feel good, and can make people happy, relaxed, and calm. Orgasms can happen alone, too, when people masturbate. Not everyone has an orgasm every time they are sexual, and what feels best for one body might not feel best for another.

There are different kinds of "having sex," and one way is when a person puts their penis inside of another person's vagina. This is a kind of sexual intercourse called *vaginal intercourse*, and it can result in a baby being made. This is where the sperm go on their journey—when a person with a penis has an orgasm, and semen is ejaculated into the vagina, the sperm travel through the uterus and fallopian tubes to find the egg (more on this in Chapter 7).

People have sex for a lot of reasons, and not only when they want to make a baby. One reason is because it feels good. The genitals have a lot of nerve endings which make them sensitive and pleasurable to touch. The clitoris is the only part of anyone's body that only functions for pleasure! If two people want to have sex and not make a baby, there are ways to keep the sperm from getting to the egg called *contraception*, also known as *birth control*. Birth control allows people to have sex just for pleasure without worrying about making a baby (more on this in Chapter 11).

Another reason people have sex is to show their love for another person. That is why sex is sometimes called "making love." Sex can come with a lot of emotions. Sex can also come with some risks, and that is why it is important for people to be mature and have a level of trust before they have sex with someone else (more on this in Chapter 11).

There are a lot of types of love that do not include sex. We can show love to people by saying "I love you," giving them a hug, or holding their hand. We can also show people we love them by cuddling or kissing them.

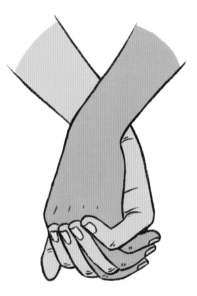

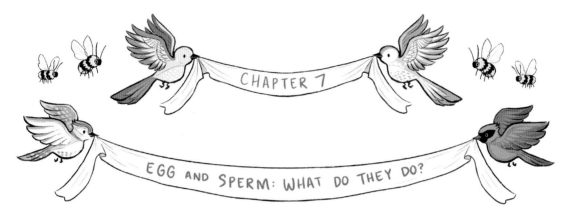

CHAPTER 7

EGG AND SPERM: WHAT DO THEY DO?

When a new baby is made by sperm and egg cells, we call it *reproduction*. *Cells* make up all human bodies, and plants and animals, too! Reproduction is how humans, plants, and animals make new humans, plants, and animals like them. In human beings, people have sex in order to help sperm and an egg meet to form a new baby. Sometimes sperm and eggs find each other with the help of a doctor (more about that in Chapter 8).

Eggs and sperm go on pretty amazing journeys to meet each other. The egg's journey starts in an ovary. After puberty begins, people who have ovaries produce a single egg once a month that comes out of the ovary and travels through one of the two fallopian tubes. If that egg meets a sperm after two people have sex, they can join together to travel to the uterus. The newly combined egg and sperm are called a *zygote*. The zygote snuggles in and makes itself at home in the uterus, where it can grow and eventually turn into a baby.

FERTILIZATION
(THE EGG'S JOURNEY)

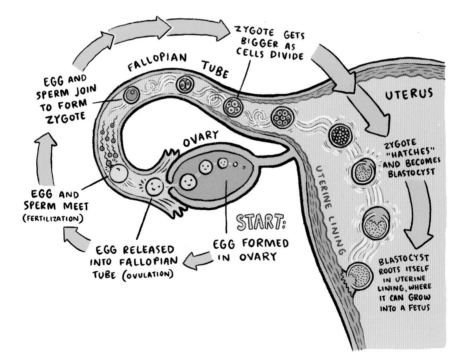

Every month another egg gets ready to leave the ovary on this same journey. The uterus makes a new lining every month, too. This lining is only needed when an egg and sperm join to make a baby. When the egg and sperm don't join, the lining becomes the menstrual blood. People who have these body parts do not begin to menstruate until after puberty begins. People usually get their first period between the ages of 8 and 15.

MENSTRUAL CYCLE
(THE EGG'S JOURNEY)

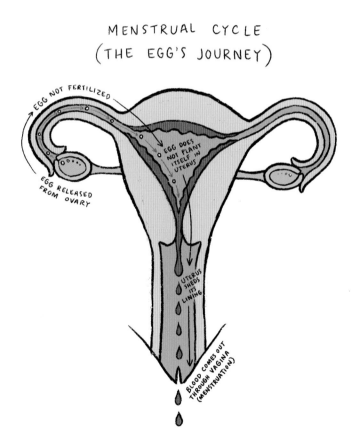

Sperm's journey begins in the testicles. When sperm are made in the testicles, they also prepare for an amazing trip. They travel to the epididymis and stay there for a few weeks to mature. Then they go on a race through the vas deferens. They pass by the seminal vesicles and the prostate gland, which adds a milky liquid to the cells. Together, the mix of sperm and liquid is called *semen*. This liquid keeps sperm energized and healthy for their race. They continue through the urethra and come out of the tip of the penis when the person has an orgasm during sex or by themselves. When sperm go on their race and do not meet an egg, no baby can be created.

EJACULATION
(THE SPERM'S JOURNEY)

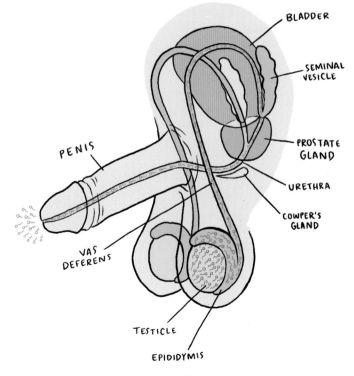

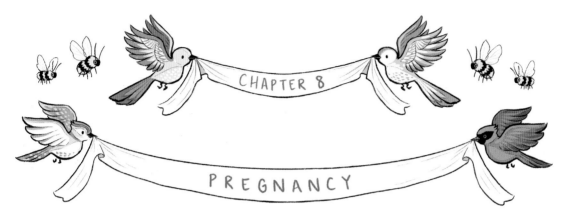

CHAPTER 8

PREGNANCY

When the sperm and egg cells join together, the fertilized egg is called a *zygote*. When the zygote travels and implants into the wall of the uterus, the group of cells is an *embryo*. The group of cells is so tiny that it's smaller than the point of a pin! When an embryo grows for three months, it is then called a *fetus*. A fetus keeps growing until it is ready to be born, and when it is born, it is a baby! A uterus is also called a *womb*. Pregnancy isn't just for women. Trans men and non-binary people with uteruses can get pregnant too! A person is pregnant once the group of cells arrives in the womb and starts to grow. During pregnancy, the uterus stretches like a balloon to make space for the fetus as it grows (but, unlike a balloon, it never bursts!). The uterus goes back to its usual size after a baby is born.

The whole pregnancy process usually takes nine months—for the embryo to become a fetus, for the fetus to grow, and for a baby to be born! Along the way, the growing fetus is very busy in the womb. It lives inside the *amniotic sac*, a fluid-filled bag inside the uterus. The fetus gets nutrients and oxygen through a soft organ called the *placenta*, which connects to the parent through the *umbilical cord*. Did you know that your belly button is where YOUR umbilical cord was attached? Food, water, and air that the parent takes into their body gets broken down into bits in their blood, and the umbilical cord brings the fetus some of these bits so that it's healthy and fed. The parent's body can bring in some unhealthy things, too: alcohol, drugs, and cigarette smoke can all be very dangerous for a fetus. Most people who get pregnant try to be very careful about what goes into their bodies, such as safe foods and safe medicines, so that they can keep their bodies healthy for the fetus.

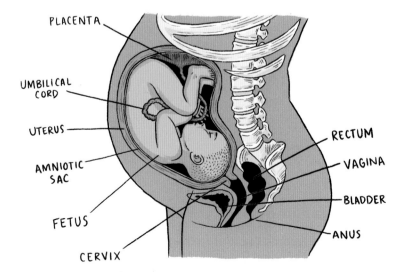

During pregnancy, the fetus kicks and moves and makes a fist. It does somersaults, tastes food, has the hiccups, and blinks its eyes. It can hear sounds from outside the uterus, too. The person who is pregnant can feel the fetus moving inside, but the movement doesn't hurt them. Once the fetus gets big enough, you might be able to see it move from the outside of the pregnant person's belly. At a doctor's appointment, the doctor can do an *ultrasound* to see pictures of the fetus inside the uterus and to check to see if it is healthy. Sometimes the doctor can tell the parents the fetus's biological sex based on the genitals that they can see in the ultrasound. The doctor can see if there is one fetus, or twins, or triplets, or even more babies growing inside.

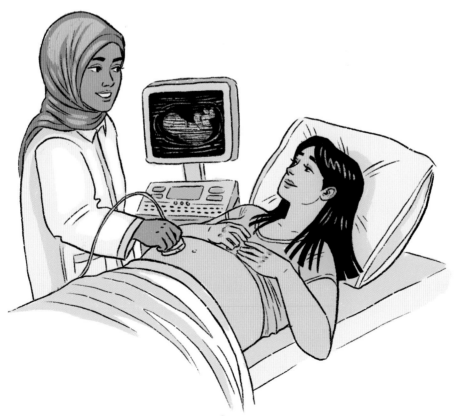

Sometimes a pregnancy can start and then end before a fetus or an embryo is healthy enough to become a baby. When a pregnancy ends with no warning, it is called a *miscarriage*. This can be very sad for pregnant people. Miscarriages are common, especially in the early stages of pregnancy. Most people who experience miscarriages can still become pregnant and give birth to a baby in the future.

Becoming a parent is a big responsibility! Some people decide they want to have babies, and some people choose not to. There are many ways for adults to be happy, and what's right for one person might not be right for another. Some people make plans for how to avoid getting pregnant at all. Some people become pregnant and choose not to stay pregnant. There are medical and surgical ways that people can end a pregnancy, called *abortion*. Some people have very strong feelings about abortion, but ending a pregnancy is a very personal decision.

FROM ZYGOTE TO FETUS

1 DAY

1 MONTH

2 MONTHS

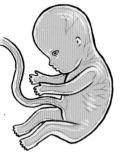

3 MONTHS

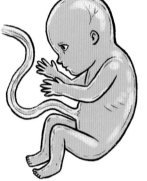

4 MONTHS

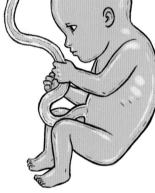

5 MONTHS

6 MONTHS

7 MONTHS

8 MONTHS

9 MONTHS

- At first, it is a ball of cells.
- Month 1: The embryo is the size of a poppy seed, and the placenta is forming.
- Month 2: The embryo is growing fingers and toes, and lots of body systems! It's as big as a kidney bean.
- Month 3: The fetus's genitals have developed, and the fetus is covered in soft hair. It's the size of a lime.
- Month 4: The fetus can suck its thumb, yawn, and stretch, and it's as big as an avocado.
- Month 5: The fetus is as long as a banana, and it is exercising its developing muscles.
- Month 6: The fetus is the size of a papaya, and might be growing some hair on its head.
- Month 7: The fetus might be moving around even more, and it's as big as an eggplant.
- Month 8: The fetus is still growing, to the size of a pineapple! It has developed lungs.
- Month 9: The fetus has less space to move around and is getting ready to be a baby! It might be facing head down to prepare for birth, and it's the size of a watermelon.

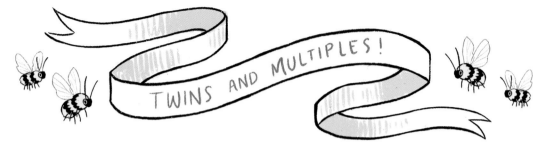

Sometimes a person is pregnant with more than one baby inside. When more than one baby is born, we call it a *multiple birth*. Two babies born together are twins. Three are called triplets. Four are called quadruplets, and five are called quintuplets!

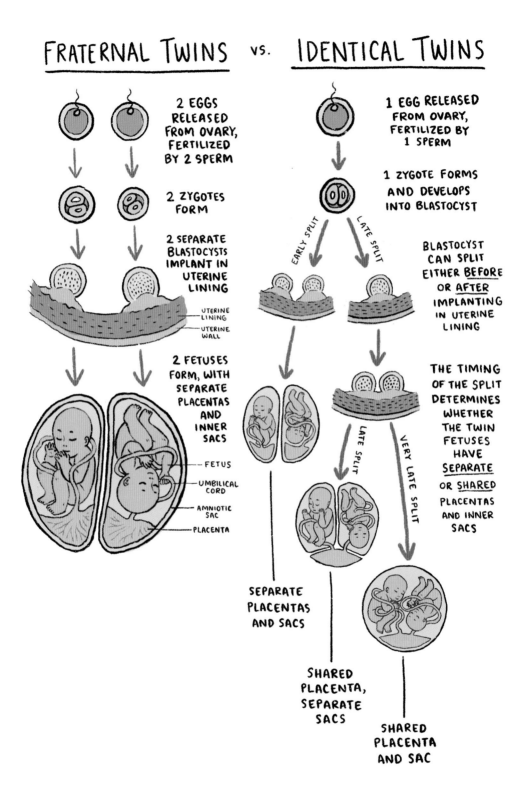

FRATERNAL TWINS vs. IDENTICAL TWINS

2 EGGS RELEASED FROM OVARY, FERTILIZED BY 2 SPERM

1 EGG RELEASED FROM OVARY, FERTILIZED BY 1 SPERM

2 ZYGOTES FORM

1 ZYGOTE FORMS AND DEVELOPS INTO BLASTOCYST

2 SEPARATE BLASTOCYSTS IMPLANT IN UTERINE LINING

UTERINE LINING
UTERINE WALL

EARLY SPLIT

LATE SPLIT

BLASTOCYST CAN SPLIT EITHER BEFORE OR AFTER IMPLANTING IN UTERINE LINING

2 FETUSES FORM, WITH SEPARATE PLACENTAS AND INNER SACS

FETUS
UMBILICAL CORD
AMNIOTIC SAC
PLACENTA

THE TIMING OF THE SPLIT DETERMINES WHETHER THE TWIN FETUSES HAVE SEPARATE OR SHARED PLACENTAS AND INNER SACS

LATE SPLIT

VERY LATE SPLIT

SEPARATE PLACENTAS AND SACS

SHARED PLACENTA, SEPARATE SACS

SHARED PLACENTA AND SAC

Identical twins are formed when one fertilized egg divides into two parts, making two separate fertilized cells. Identical twins share all of the same genes and have the same biological sex, and they look very much alike! They are also called *monozygotic* because they come from one fertilized egg, or zygote. Some identical twins share the same placenta and amniotic sac, and some have their own placenta and sac.

Fraternal twins occur when two eggs are released during ovulation. These are *dizygotic* twins because they come from two separate zygotes. These twins do not share the exact same mix of genes, and might not share the same biological sex. These twins usually have their own placenta and amniotic sac.

The chances of being a twin are about 3 in 100. It is even rarer to be an identical twin, and super rare to be a triplet.

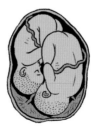

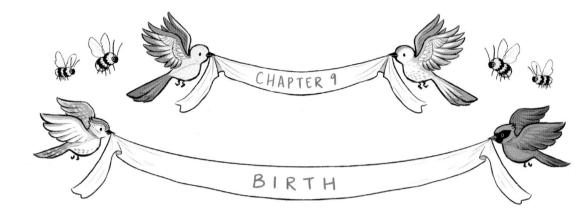

CHAPTER 9

BIRTH

When a baby is ready to be born, the uterus starts to squeeze and contract. These contractions of the uterus mean that the pregnant person is *in labor* and ready to push the baby out of their vagina. Labor and birth can happen at home, at a birth center, or at a hospital. Lots of people can help a baby to be born, such as a doctor or a specialist called a *midwife*. Labor can take just a few hours or it could take more than a day. The muscles of the uterus work hard and the vagina stretches wide to fit the baby through.

When the baby comes out of the vagina, the midwife or the doctor holds the baby and someone cuts the umbilical cord that connects the baby to their parent. The cord was what helped the fetus eat and breathe, but now most babies can do this on their own. In about a week, the little part of the umbilical cord left on the baby falls off, and the place where the cord was cut becomes the baby's belly button! When the baby cries for the first time, air gets into their lungs and they can start breathing air. When the baby is born, their parents are able to hold them for the first time. This is an exciting moment!

After a couple of minutes, the placenta has to come through the vagina, too. The parent does not need the placenta to help a fetus eat and breathe anymore, so it passes through the body after the baby is born.

C-SECTION
SCAR

If the parent is having trouble pushing the baby from their uterus or something makes it unsafe to push the baby out, the doctor might have to deliver the baby another way. This can happen for a lot of reasons—if the baby is too big, or is not in the right position, or if the baby is not moving down fast enough. A doctor might need to make a cut into the parent's body to get the baby from their uterus, in a surgery called a *cesarean section* or *c-section*. The parent gets medicine so that they can't feel the cut, and the baby is taken out to be born. Then the doctor removes the placenta and sews the uterus and the belly back up! This is another way that babies can be born, and it is completely normal.

Most fetuses take the whole nine months to grow inside the womb. But some babies are born early, and these babies are called *premature* or *preemie*. Sometimes these babies need to stay in the hospital to help them gain weight and keep growing. The baby can go home once they are big enough and strong enough.

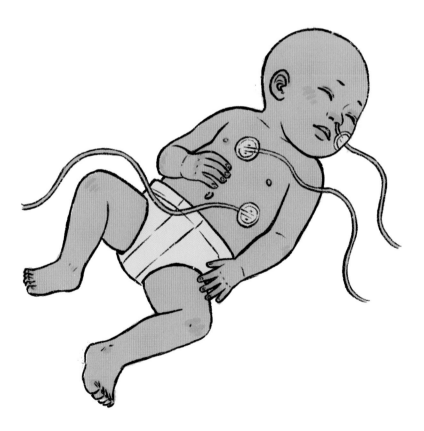

Now that the baby is born, they need food. After a parent gives birth, their body can create milk in their breasts. A baby *nurses*, or sucks and drinks milk from their parent's breast, and the breasts make more milk. Have you ever seen other animals feeding their babies by allowing them to nurse? *Breastmilk* has all of the nutrients and vitamins that the baby needs, and is all the nourishment a baby needs in their first few months of life. Brand-new babies need to be fed very often!

Some parents feed the babies from their breasts, and some feed the babies from a bottle. Parents who do not feed babies from their breasts feed babies with *formula*. Formula is different from breast milk, and a baby can drink it from a bottle. Formula can also have all of the nutrients and vitamins that the baby needs to be healthy. Babies can start to eat other foods after several months.

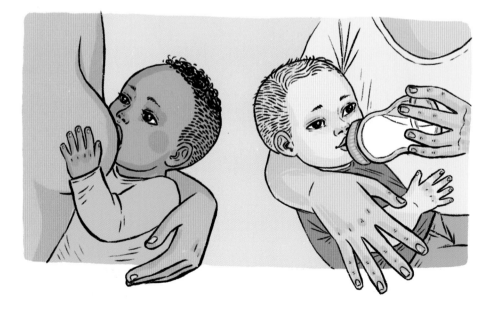

If there is a new baby in your family, you might have a lot of feelings—you might be excited, nervous, or both! You might be jealous that the baby gets a lot of attention, or bored when the baby can't do everything that you can do. But being with babies can be fun, too, and they learn a lot by watching you! You can sing, make funny faces, or talk to a baby. You can read to a baby, hold them gently, and make art for the baby to look at. If you don't always feel like playing with the baby, or feel upset with them sometimes, that's normal too.

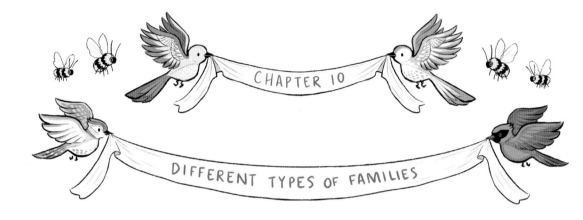

CHAPTER 10

There are all sorts of families in the world. Some have a mom and a dad, some have two moms, and some have two dads. Some have parents who are non-binary, some have a single parent. Some families have a stepparent, some have aunts and uncles, and some have grandparents and great-grandparents! Some people have parents who are married and some people have parents who are separated or divorced.

Parents, siblings, grandparents, aunts, uncles, cousins, and other relatives and friends can all be part of a person's family. And there are lots of ways to add babies to a family!

If one parent has a body that makes sperm, and one parent has a body that makes an egg, the sperm and egg can join and grow in a uterus to make a baby.

Sometimes two people who want to be parents have the body parts to join the sperm and egg, but pregnancy does not happen for them. They might try and try, but lots of things can make having a baby difficult for their bodies. A doctor can sometimes help them become pregnant by taking the sperm and egg and joining them outside the bodies in a little petri dish, and then implanting the joined cells into a parent's uterus so that a baby can grow. This is called *in vitro fertilization* (IVF).

Sometimes two people who want to be parents have body parts that are not able to join a sperm and egg, so they might use a *donor*, or a person who donates their sperm or egg to help a baby grow. If neither of those two people have a uterus, they might use a *surrogate*, or someone who grows the baby in their uterus for two people who want to have a baby.

IN VITRO FERTILIZATION

SPERM

EGGS

Sometimes people who have a baby cannot take care of a baby and make a plan for that baby to be taken care of by other people. Some babies and kids live with other family members that are not their biological parents. Others are *fostered* and live with people until their parents can take care of a child again. When biological parents cannot take care of a baby, they might plan for the baby to be *adopted* by people who want to be their forever parents, who will love and raise that child as their child.

Parents can adopt children if they can't make a baby with their bodies. Parents can also adopt children if they can make or have made a baby with their bodies. Parents can adopt a baby in their own country, or they can adopt a baby from another place in the world! The most important thing is for parents to be able to care for, love, and support their children.

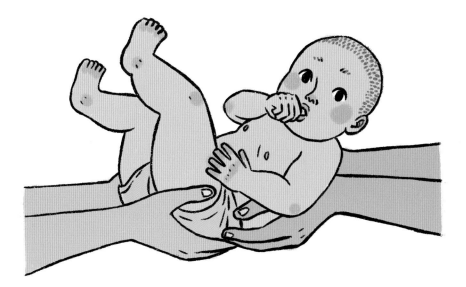

People who are born from their parents' bodies can look alike because they share some of the same genes. Even if a baby doesn't share the same genes as their parents, they might share some of their habits or likes, because we learn a lot from our parents.

Some people have parents that are lesbian, gay, bisexual, or queer. Sometimes people have parents who are transgender. Other people who are not LGBTQIA are not always kind to families that are different, sometimes because they don't understand, and sometimes because they got the idea that these different families are wrong for being who they are. Love and kindness are important, and if we don't understand something, we can be kind first and ask questions later!

CHAPTER 11

KEEPING YOUR BODY SAFE

ots of people like hugs, kisses, tickles, and cuddles from people who love them! These are *good touches*. It is important to ask before we touch other people because everyone is the boss of their own body. Usually, we need to ask permission for lots of things—if we can borrow a toy, if we can pet a dog, and if we can give someone a cuddle. This is called *asking for consent*. If someone says, "Yes, I would love to have a hug," this is called *giving consent*. People can change their minds about what they want for their bodies. When someone says "NO" or "DON'T" or "STOP," we should not continue to touch their bodies.

WORDS THAT ARE ALWAYS OK TO SAY:

This counts for you, too! If you decide someone is touching your body and you do not want them to—even if that someone is someone you know or love—you can say "NO" or "DON'T" or "STOP." If that person does not stop touching your body, that is *bad touching*. Even if someone tells you that touching your body is a secret and not to tell anyone else, you should tell an adult that you trust, such as a doctor, a teacher, or someone in your family. If the first person does not believe you, keep telling until someone listens. Forcing anyone to touch or be touched is wrong. If someone touches your body when you don't want them to, you might feel a lot of strong feelings like fear, sadness, embarrassment, or anger. These are normal reactions, and it's important to tell a grown-up you trust about them.

Other people that may need to check our bodies to make sure they are healthy are a nurse and doctor, or maybe a parent. Otherwise, our genitals are private and are no one else's business. Some people think asking about people's genitals is okay, especially when it comes to transgender people. It is not appropriate for any adult to ask about your genitals, unless you are getting a check-up at the doctor's office. You do not need to tell anyone about your private parts if they do ask. You can talk to trusted adults about questions you have about genitals. When your body starts to change during puberty, it might mean that you want to get dressed by yourself, or keep your body more private than you used to. Privacy means you get to say who sees your body.

Another big part of keeping our bodies safe is to know some of the risks of sexual activity. Just as we can catch someone else's cold when they are sick, we can also share *sexually transmitted infections* (STIs) from being sexual with other people. These infections spread through oral, vaginal, or anal sex. Some of these infections are from bacteria and some are from viruses. Some can be treated and cured, and some can't. Some have signs and symptoms, where we see or feel that something is wrong in our bodies, but many don't! Not having sex, or *abstinence*, is the only 100% way of preventing STIs. But the best way to keep bodies safe when people decide to be sexual is to get tested by doctors—and to use condoms the right way, every time. *External condoms* are thin covers that protect the penis and make sure the semen and skin don't share STIs.

There are also *internal condoms* that protect the vagina and the anus. Condoms also prevent sex from leading to pregnancy by making sure the sperm do not go into the other person to meet the egg.

Many people have sex but don't want to make a baby, and there are lots of ways to keep the sperm from reaching the egg. These ways are called *birth control* or *contraception*. They include things like condoms, pills, and injections. If someone wants to have sex without ever making a baby, they might choose to have a surgery to block the path of sperm or an egg.

Doctors and trusted adults can help you find more information about how people keep their bodies safe in sexual situations.

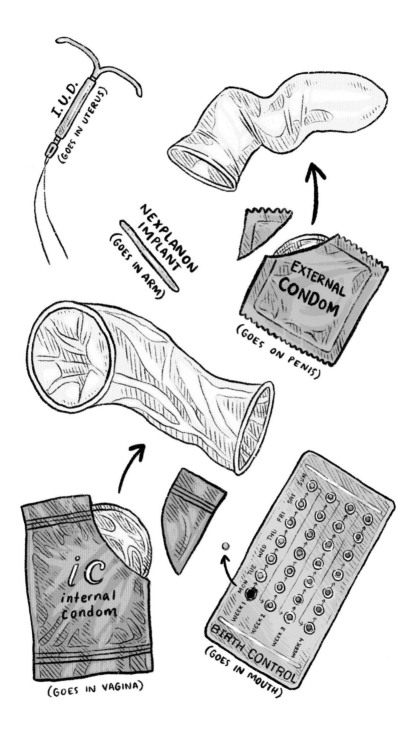

RESPECTING EACH OTHER

Some people think genitals decide our gender, and that people with penises can only be boys, and people with vulvas can only be girls. What body parts you have, which bathroom you use, and whether you are transgender or cisgender is private, and you don't have to tell strangers this information! If someone tells someone else about your genitals or whether you are transgender, and you did not share that information yourself, this can be called *outing*. We do not want to out other people, because everyone deserves privacy, and they need to consent to share that information. Sometimes, others think that they know a person's gender identity, or whether they are transgender, based on what their eyes see. But that's not always accurate! If you're not sure whether someone uses "he" or "she" or "they," you can always just ask what pronouns they use. It's not appropriate to assume or ask if someone is transgender based on the way they look, and it's always your choice what information you share with other people.

CHAPTER 12

SEX IN THE MEDIA

The *media* we see includes TV, movies, music, magazines, books, podcasts, advertisements, and the internet. Sometimes in the media, there are things for grown-ups that aren't for kids. Your parents have probably told you that you can't watch something because it is violent or maybe has sex scenes. The media also shows us less obvious sexual messages all the time, even towards young people. Some of these messages end up being really unhealthy or unrealistic, and get in the way of having healthy ideas about our bodies and sexuality.

Some of the messages we get tell us which body types, hair, and skin colors are considered "sexy." There are some messages about kids and teens needing to act sexy, too. It's important to remember that all bodies are good bodies, and that what is sexy to one person might not be sexy to another person. Sometimes it seems as if everyone else is doing something we're not, and that can pressure people to make choices they are not comfortable with in order to fit in.

When we watch sexual scenes or hear sexual stories in our media, it is important to ask lots of questions about what we see. Did the partners use protection for their bodies? Did the partners talk about what they felt comfortable doing, or did they just do it? Did anyone ask for consent to touch the other person? How do these partners treat each other? What ideas do we get about gender from these relationships? Are we seeing lots of different body sizes represented? Are there lots of people of different races? Are there people in queer relationships? What you see in the media is probably only a small example of all the many ways people are sexual or experience their gender and sexuality.

Pornography (or *porn*) is another part of human sexuality and desire, but it is not made for kids. Porn is photos or videos of sexual acts or naked bodies that is made to bring about sexual feelings in our minds and bodies. It is often found on the internet. It is normal to have these feelings, or be "turned on" by porn, but porn can give young people some of the wrong ideas about what real sex is actually like with another person. It can give us unrealistic expectations of people's bodies, the sexual activity they want, and whose pleasure is most important. It also doesn't include communication between partners very often.

If you end up seeing something on the internet that was not made for kids, it might make you feel uncomfortable, confused, or grossed out. It also might make you feel excited and curious. If you are ever online and find yourself receiving uncomfortable information, talking to a trusted adult can help keep you safe online.

Adults sometime use phones and the internet to feel sexy. Sending sexual messages isn't safe for kids. Sending sexual pictures of a kid is against the law and can get people into a lot of trouble! Not everyone you meet on the internet is who they say they are, and once something is online, it is online forever. If you feel upset or confused about what someone asks you online, listen to what your gut tells you about the choices you are making. Listening to yourself and thinking about your values are really powerful tools, and you can use them to make and communicate the right choices to keep you safe.

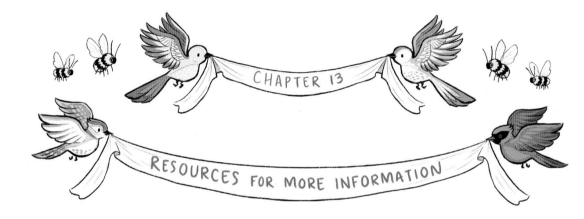

CHAPTER 13

RESOURCES FOR MORE INFORMATION

This book has a lot of information in it, but there's so much more out there. If you have more questions, I hope you'll be able to talk to a parent, doctor, therapist, teacher, school counselor, or other trusted adult. There are also so many wonderful resources that are doing the great work of comprehensive sexuality education, providing information, and creating community. Here are some places to go for further education, guidance, and support:

ACLU Guide for Supporting Transgender Students
www.aclu.org/report/schools-transition

Advocates for Youth
www.advocatesforyouth.org

Amaze
www.amaze.org

Bish Training
https://bishtraining.com

Brook
https://www.brook.org.uk

DO SRE For Schools
https://www.dosreforschools.com

Gender Spectrum
www.genderspectrum.org

GLSEN
www.glsen.org

HRC's Welcoming Schools Foundation
www.welcomingschools.org

I Wanna Know
www.iwannaknow.org

PFLAG
https://pflag.org

Planned Parenthood
www.plannedparenthood.org

Queer Kid Stuff
www.queerkidstuff.com

Scarleteen
www.scarleteen.com

Sex Education Forum
https://www.sexeducationforum.org.uk

Sex, Etc.
www.sexetc.org

Sex Positive Families
www.sexpositivefamilies.com

Sexuality Information and Education Council of the United States (SIECUS)
www.siecus.org

Talk With Your Kids
www.talkwithyourkids.org

Teaching Sexual Health
www.teachingsexualhealth.ca

Teaching Tolerance
www.tolerance.org

ACKNOWLEDGEMENTS

This book could not exist without the support and encouragement of so many people, or without collaborative partnerships with some amazing organizations. I am so grateful for the irreplaceable staff at the Gender and Sexuality Clinic at CHOP. Dr. Linda Hawkins and Dr. Nadia Dowshen, the world is a better place because of your work. Thanks to Dr. Alison Myers and the clinicians at Penn Family Medicine. Thanks to Dr. Danna Bodenheimer and the staff of the Walnut Psychotherapy Center for providing a space for clients and clinicians alike to grow and explore.

I would love to thank my supervisors, mentors, and colleagues. I would not be the clinician or educator I am without Katelyn Regan, LCSW, MEd, and Dr. Sophie Fink, PsyD; thank you for being such brilliant examples. Special thanks to Katelyn for her consultation on the Special Section in Chapter 4. Marc, Robyn, Colette: I am appreciative of all that I've learned and continue to learn from each of you. Lots of thanks to the Mirons, to Ira Miller, and to WHC for encouraging my love for these topics, first as a learner and later as an educator.

To the kids, adolescents, young adults, and families that have allowed me to be a part of their journeys as their therapist: thank you for being you, in all of your authentic ways. You are the foundation for this book.

Deepest gratitude to everyone at Jessica Kingsley Publishers, including the incomparable David Corey, who has been an advocate for this book since the beginning. To Andrew James, Simeon, Hannah, Katelynn, Carolyn, Julia, and the whole editorial team: you are the greatest. Thank you for imagining this project with me.

Special thank you to Noah Grigni, who is an ineffable illustrator and a wonderful force of good and beauty in this world. Their art is what brought this book to life and I will be forever grateful for their collaboration. I could not remain afloat without the help of Jabari Lyles. Thank you for everything.

To Caitlin and Kara: there aren't enough words in the dictionary to express my gratitude for you both. You are my support in everything, and I am endlessly thankful for your patience, your long-distance presence, and your validation. I am the luckiest.

Thanks to my amazing parents who took me to the library and read me books about sexuality when I asked you questions. Nancy and Rick: thank you for helping me understand how important these topics are. To Josh, who was my first example of self-discovery: my life is so much richer because you are my family. To Brandon, Sara, and Todd, Tina, Hillary, Skip, and to my extended family: it is so amazing to have such an encouraging tribe. Special thanks to Nat, I couldn't have done it without you.

And finally, to Andrew, for telling me I could. For pushing me, for encouraging me, and for believing in this book more than anyone, I'll never stop being grateful. Thank you for being my biggest cheerleader, my toughest editor, and my constant sounding board. Your curiosity for new information is an inspiration.

This book is possible because of queer and trans people of color who have fought to be safe, seen, and known. Please consider donating to The Sylvia Rivera Law Project, Trans Lifeline, Trans Justice Funding Project, and your local LGBTQ+ center.

THE END